WRECKS AND RESCUES:
Shelter from the Storm

Wreck of the Rupert, *Tynemouth.*

WRECKS AND RESCUES:
Shelter from the Storm

A history of maritime disasters and heroism in Tyne & Wear

by

Alison Gale

© Keepdate Publishing/Alison Gale

Published by:
Keepdate (Publishing) Ltd
21 Portland Terrace
Jesmond
Newcastle upon Tyne
NE2 1QQ

First edition 1993

ISBN 0-9520494-4-9

Designed & typeset by Keepdate Ltd
Newcastle upon Tyne

Printed by The Alden Press, Oxford

PICTURE ACKNOWLEDGEMENTS

Newcastle upon Tyne City Libraries & Arts;
   Cover, pages (i), 3, 4, 7, 16, 18, 21.

Tyne & Wear Museums;
   page 11.

South Tyneside Metropolitan Borough Council;
   pages 12, 13, 17, 22, 28.

Shields Gazette;
   page 31.

North Tyneside Metropolitan Borough Council;
   pages 26, 27, 32.

© M W Marshall;
   page 40.

CONTENTS

SAFETY FROM THE STORM: Lights and Wrecks	1
LIGHTS IN THE DARKNESS	2
BIRTH OF THE LIFEBOAT	5
ROCKET MEN: The Volunteer Life Brigades	10
SURVIVAL AND GROWTH: Lifeboat Services	17
HAZARDS TO HAVENS: New Piers and Lighthouses	21
TREND-SETTING: Tynemouth's Motor Lifeboat Rescues	25
ON COURSE FOR THE MODERN WORLD	29
DIVING INTO THE PAST	34
LOOKING AROUND	35
FURTHER READING	39

SAFETY FROM THE STORM:
Lights and Wrecks

The entrances of the rivers Tyne and Wear were once the graveyards of many fine sailing ships – their hulls taking in water and masts toppling as they failed to claw their way off the rocks and treacherous, shifting sand banks that littered the river mouths.

The rivers, now quiet, were once busy with sailing ships. For centuries coal was carried from the North East to London and sand and shingle taken on board as ballast for the return voyage. On arrival, the ballast was dumped in the lower reaches of the rivers to make way for the cargo of coal. The rivers became even more dangerous and shallow as the ballast added to existing sandbanks.

As early as the sixteenth century these colliers were regularly leaving the two rivers, braving their river mouths and heading out to the open sea. Their voyage down the North East coast to London was never easy – sudden storms were a constant threat. In 1695 a severe gale struck and 200 Tyne vessels were wrecked.

For a North East sailor death by drowning was never far away. The Tyne river mouth was blocked by a sand bank (the bar) which could only be crossed at high tide and only local knowledge could find the ever-changing narrow channel. One slip of navigation, one misinterpreted order and the North Sea's relentless waves and strong easterly winds would drive a sailing ship off course. The result – a grounding: to the north, the terrible Black Middens Rocks; to the south, the notorious Herd Sands. Pounded by the heavy breakers, ships soon disappeared without trace.

Powerless from the shore, and time and time again silent witnesses to tragic disasters, the

people of the North East finally decided to reduce the suffering and toll on seamen's lives. Their new life-saving ideas were soon to be found around the coast of Britain and, not long after, along the coasts of the world. It was the people of the North East who helped give seamen a chance of safety from the storms.

LIGHTS IN THE DARKNESS

For a long time there had been some attempts to guide the sailors through the river entrances. At North Shields, for example, there are two white towers – the High and Low Lights. For ships at sea they are 'leading marks' which can be lined up to guide a vessel into the Tyne. Medieval sailors built the original towers and, at night, kept candles burning in their tops – creating the first 'leading lights' in Britain.

Henry VIII gave permission to build these High and Low Lights to the Brethren of Trinity House, Newcastle. The members of this organisation were mariners and regulated shipping on the Tyne and, sensibly, they ensured that the towers were sturdily built of stone and the windows glazed to keep the candles from blowing out. In return for building and maintaining the lights the King

allowed them to collect a toll from each ship entering the Tyne. This was called lightage; English ships paid 2d, foreign ships 4d.

Unfortunately, the changing position of the river mouth forced Trinity House to realign the High and Low lights. In 1658 new timber towers were built in the hope that they would be less costly to move around. These were replaced in 1727 with stone buildings, which in turn became redundant and new lights had to be built in 1805. Oil lamps had been used in place of candles since 1773.

Trinity House was not alone in providing lights. Tynemouth Priory had traditionally kept a coal fire burning as a warning light. Standing high on the headland to the north of the River Tyne it was visible far out to sea.

In 1664 a new tower was built using stone from the ruined priory. It stood over 79 ft (23 m) high and its square base was home to the light keeper and his family. It was the keeper's job to ensure that the coal fire burned brightly in all weathers; any smoke would

Tynemouth Lighthouse was built in 1664. Its light, a brightly burning coal fire, guided ships into the river until 1898.

Viewed from the sea (c1860), Tynemouth Lighthouse on the headland above the river mouth. It was built in 1664 using stone from the ruined priory where a light had traditionally been kept to guide ships approaching the Tyne.

obscure its light. The Tynemouth lighthouse keeper was fortunate that his lighthouse, unlike many others, had a roofed top and the fire was enclosed apart from an opening to seaward.

The Tynemouth Lighthouse was finally demolished in 1898 when new lights were built on St Mary's Island to the north and on Lizard Point – Souter Lighthouse – between the Tyne and the Wear.

BIRTH OF THE LIFEBOAT

A ship aground in the Tyne or the Wear immediately became a public spectacle. From the shore local towns-people could see the ship break up and the crew struggle to survive – it made a gruesome spectacle. It was a sufficiently common occurrence that a sailor's life was considered cheap and death unremarkable. The loss of a vessel so near to home was, however, a dramatic and highly visible blow to any struggling shipowner.

After many such disasters, the loss of one more local vessel spurred the shipowners of South Shields into action. It was on the 14th March 1789 and a northerly gale was blowing as a fleet of colliers arrived off the Tyne. Onlookers soon realised that one ship, the Newcastle-owned brig *Adventure*, had failed to follow the others into the safety of the river.

For more than 24 hours the crew bravely fought to bring their small sailing ship over the shallow bar but to no avail – the ferocious wind and sea eventually drove the *Adventure* on to the Herd Sands.

The seas were so large that even the local fishermen, who were used to rescuing sailors from ships stranded on Herd Sands, could not launch their cobles through the breakers. They could only watch as the waves pounded the *Adventure* to pieces. Only five of her thirteen man crew survived; they were miraculously washed ashore clinging to wreckage.

Following the loss of the *Adventure* the leaders of the South Shields shipowning community – known as the Gentleman of Lawe House after their traditional meeting place – advertised a prize of two guineas for a model of a boat which could be launched into large waves for the purpose of saving lives from wrecked ships. Controversially the Gentlemen of Lawe House did not choose an outright winner. Instead they commissioned one entrant, Henry Greathead, to build a vessel to their own plans and so provided South Shields with its first specially designed and purpose-built lifeboat.

The 28 ft 6 in. (8.7 m) long boat combined old and new ideas. Like the local inshore fishing boats, the coble, she had a sharp bow – a bonus for launching through surf – and was strongly built of overlapping planks (clinker). Her distinctive appearance came from a curved keel, a broad cork belt outside her gunwale for buoyancy and her double ends which meant that she could be rowed in either direction. She was pulled through the water by five pairs of oars, with two men on each oar, and was steered by a sweeping oar in the bow and the stern.

This dramatic engraving of a Greathead-type lifeboat shows the crew, two to an oar, battling through enormous waves beneath Tynemouth Lighthouse.

Any doubts over the seaworthiness of the new boat, which came to be called the *Original*, were soon dismissed. *Original*'s first rescue was made in a blizzard when the crew of a sloop, grounded on Herd Sands, was brought safely ashore. In the next eight years the lifeboat and her crew supported by the Tyne Lifeboat Institution were to save 200 lives.

One memorable night in 1798 the Duke of Northumberland watched as the lifeboat crew tirelessly went off the shore in a violent storm to four wrecks, successively bringing ashore the crews. The men of the *Gateshead*, the *Planter*, the *Beaver* and the *Mary* owed their lives to the brave lifeboatmen. The Tyne Lifeboat Institution already had hopes for building a second lifeboat and when the Duke, so impressed by the effectiveness of the rescue operation, offered to fund the second boat they gratefully accepted. In November 1798 the second lifeboat, the *Northumberland*, made her first rescue, saving six lives from the *Edinburgh* aground on the Herd Sands.

The story of the South Shields' lifeboats spread around Britain and, through seamen, to other countries. Soon many places wanted lifeboats and Henry Greathead built 35 between 1798 and 1810. Additional boats were built by other people under licence.

The entrance to the river Wear had, like the Tyne, claimed many seamen's lives and the Wearsiders, as appalled by the loss of life as the Tynesiders, soon had their own lifeboat. In 1799 Sunderland formed a lifeboat committee after one more terrible local shipwreck and a Greathead-type lifeboat was built by local boatbuilder William Wake of Bishopswearmouth. In 1811 the Sunderland Committee, full of new ideas, fitted their lifeboat with airtight compartments to increase its buoyancy.

By the 1820s many places had lifeboats but funding was often a problem – few had copied the sound organisation of the Tyne Lifeboat Institution. Consequently, public support was canvassed for a national body to fund and operate lifeboat stations and, in 1824, the National Society for Preservation of Life From Shipwreck was created. In 1854 the National Society became first the National Lifeboat Institution and, within weeks of its conception, the Institution added Royal to its title to become the famous Royal National Lifeboat Institution (RNLI).

The Tyne Lifeboat Institution, along with many other stations, remained independent of the new national body. After the *Original* was damaged, the Port of Tyne branch of the national society, seeing the town's difficulty in financing a new boat, offered to raise the funds and bring the station under its auspices. The offer was spurned and local fundraising brought the new lifeboat *Tyne* on station in mid-1833. South Shields was enormously proud of it.

ROCKET MEN:
The Volunteer Life Brigades

In 1809 a major step forward in ship to shore rescue was made off Yarmouth. A local artillery officer, George Manby, who was experimenting with mortars which carried lines to stricken vessels so that their crew could be hauled ashore, fired his lines over the Sunderland collier *Nancy* when she was driven ashore. The startled crew were all saved, and the new lifesaving equipment was soon in use all round the British coast.

Supported by the government George Manby toured the country demonstrating his Life-saving Apparatus (LSA) which was quickly supplied to all the Coastguard Stations. The mortars carried a light line to the ship in distress. The line was attached to a strong hawser which was pulled out to form a link between the ship and the shore. The crew were then lifted off in a cradle which was hauled back and forth along the hawser.

The Tynemouth Coastguards were soon in action with 'Manby Mortars' as they became known. In 1830 the South Shields Gazette reported that the lifeboat *Original*, while taking crew off the stranded *Gratton*, had been driven inshore by a wave. As the boat was dragged across the Black Middens, the back of the boat had been broken. The *Gratton*'s remaining crew were brought off the ship with the new LSA.

Soon new rockets invented by John Dennett replaced the Manby Mortars. The Society for Preservation of Life from Shipwreck, always open to new ideas, provided the North East with these new Dennett rockets which were much easier to carry and more accurate than Manby Mortars.

Rescue with LSA. A crewman is suspended in the breeches buoy which hangs beneath the hawser running from the ship to the shore. He is hauled ashore by the team of four men pulling on the line (whip). In the foreground is the rocket launching tripod.

The position of this ship shows the danger faced by crews caught between the sea and rugged cliffs. The PC 71 stranded against Trow Rocks in November 1923.

Another new lifesaving invention was a special rope ladder devised by Mr. Moffat of North Shields. The ladders were desperately needed as ships were sometimes driven ashore against the steep cliffs that lay between the Tyne and the Wear. Whole crews had been washed off to their deaths as they tried to scramble up the cliffs to safety. The Society for Preservation of Life from Shipwreck soon provided the new rope ladders to help rescuers reach ships on the beaches.

Coordinated teamwork was becoming increasingly important in rescue operations. Coastguards and lifeboatmen worked together and the rescue from the *Fowlis* in 1861 remains a remarkable demonstration of their teamwork. The wind was too strong for rockets to be fired from the pier at South Shields and the water was too shallow for the lifeboats to approach the stricken vessel. The coastguards

The schooner William *resting on the Herd Sands in July 1919. Her crew were taken off by South Shields VLB when she was driven ashore in a gale. The VLB Watch House can be seen in the distance beneath her bowsprit.*

were taken aboard the lifeboat *Tyne* and rowed to windward of the wreck. In the rolling waves just outside the breaking surf rockets were fired over the ship and her crew were pulled into the lifeboat using the special cradle or 'breeches buoy' of the LSA.

In November 1864 the *SS Stanley* put into the Tyne to shelter from bad weather, but she was caught by heavy seas and driven on to the angry rocks of the Black Middens. Four lifeboats – *Northumberland*, *Tyne*, *Providence*, and *Constance*, an RNLI boat stationed at Tynemouth – were already in action taking crew off stranded sailing vessels. But the violence of the seas and shallowness of the water prevented any lifeboat reaching the *Stanley*.

Hampered by onlookers and contending with strong winds the Tynemouth Coastguards set up their LSA. Four people were brought ashore but two died as they were hauled through the huge waves and over the jagged rocks. Not surprisingly, many passengers were afraid to risk the breeches buoy, and when the equipment jammed they had no hope of rescue. While the coastguards sent to Cullercoats for more LSA the crowd watched helplessly as the ship broke in two. When the rescue resumed five crew and some 20 passengers had been lost.

Captain Morrison, stationed in Tynemouth Castle, suggested that local people be trained to 'help rather than hinder' the coastguard. The Mayor of Tynemouth called a public meeting and the Tynemouth Volunteer Life Brigade was quickly formed with 220 willing members. The Board of Trade endorsed the new body and supplied LSA with the improved Boxer rockets which replaced the Dennett version.

The Tynemouth concept of a Volunteer Life Brigade spread so rapidly that although Tynemouth had been the first British town to form a Brigade it was deprived of making the first Volunteer Life Brigade rescue. The honour went to South Shields for rescuing the crew of the *Tenterden* with its master and his wife and child in April 1866, just two months after their Volunteer Life Brigade was formed.

Sunderland formed a Volunteer Life Brigade in March 1877. There were so many volunteers that the Brigade was divided into five companies, three on the south side of the harbour and two on the north. Their first rescue came seven months later when 19 crew men were brought ashore from the *Loch Cree*.

The Brigadesmen were dedicated and hardy. In the most foul weather they kept all-night watches with no shelter except the wave-lashed parapets of the piers. Public admiration for their work soon turned to financial support and enabled them to build special Watch Houses. These can still be seen at Cullercoats (built 1879), Tynemouth (1868), South Shields (1867) and Roker (1905 – replacing an earlier building).

By the twentieth century some 5000 volunteers were serving in approximately 400 Volunteer Life Brigades around the coast of Britain.

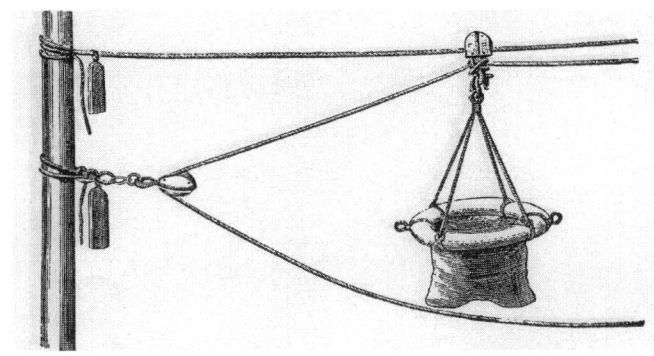

Breeches buoy

Crowds watching the Diamante *on the rocks at Spanish Battery Point, March 1898. As the barque crossed the bar, a wave broke over her stern damaging her steering gear. Once disabled, she was driven ashore.*

Local people looking around the schooner William *after she went aground on the Herd Sands in July 1919.*

WRECKS AND RESCUES

The twisted wreck of the Fame, *in 1894, draws people onto the rocks at Tynemouth.*

SURVIVAL AND GROWTH:
Lifeboat Services

In 1849 the loss of a Tyne lifeboat was national news. The disaster shocked the country and people expressed their grief by pledging support for lifeboats. Ironically it was not the Tyne Lifeboat Institution who benefited but the national body, the Society for the Preservation of Life from Shipwreck.

The freak accident occurred during the December gales. The lifeboat *Providence* had been launched in heavy seas to assist the *Betsy* which was aground on the Herd Sands. Just after her crew had skilfully laid her alongside the ship a wave ran between the two vessels and overturned the lifeboat. The crew of the *Betsy* pulled one lifeboatman to safety and could see another three on the upturned boat.

The crowds ashore rushed to launch the *Tyne*. After bringing the crew of the *Betsy* and the four lifeboatmen ashore, she joined the *Northumberland* in searching the wild waters for the *Providence* and her crew. When the two crews towed their sister lifeboat ashore the crowds waded into the water to turn her upright. She was completely empty. Twenty of her 24 man crew had drowned.

The Duke of Northumberland harnessed the support created by the *Providence* tragedy when he became President of the National Society, which he reorganised as the Royal National Lifeboat Institution (RNLI). In 1851 he offered a prize for the design of a new lifeboat. Over 30 of the 200 entries were sent by builders and inventors on the Tyne and the Wear. The committee which judged the competition also prepared plans for a new lifeboat for use throughout the country. They were eager to learn from the misfortune of the *Providence*, and for this reason favoured a boat which would right itself in the event of a capsize.

In 1862 a Newcastle banker provided the RNLI with its first Tyne-based lifeboat. He bought one of the RNLI's new boats which he named *Constance* after his wife, and placed it in a new lifeboat house in Prior's Haven at Tynemouth. Three years later a second RNLI station was opened on the Black Middens first for the *Pomfret-Goole* and then two later lifeboats, each named *Forester*. The station was closed in 1905 after a motor lifeboat was provided for the Tyne.

Shortly after establishing its Tynemouth station, the RNLI began work in Sunderland where the sailors and shipowners had separately maintained a number of independent lifeboats since 1800. In 1864 two of the five Sunderland based lifeboats were in poor repair and the RNLI was asked to provide a replacement. They sent the self-righting *Florence Nightingale* which served the port until 1892. In 1871 the shipowners also placed their three lifeboats under the control of the RNLI. Until the end of the nineteenth century there were three lifeboat stations within the Wear and a fourth at the south outlet where the docks opened to the North Sea.

The Tyne Lifeboat Institution had the confidence to remain both independent of the RNLI and faithful to their original design of oared lifeboats. Prior to 1849 when disaster struck and the *Providence* was lost with most of its crew the Tyne Lifeboat Institution had enjoyed 60 years of remarkable achievement. During this period they had never lost a lifeboatman and only the *Original* had been retired through damage. Three lifeboats were in operation; the *Providence*, which had been brought into service in 1842, the *Tyne* in 1833 and the *Northumberland* 1798. Between 1841 and 1849 these boats had saved 466 lives.

In the 1870s the Tyne fleet was extended to four boats, Tom Perry replacing *Providence*, which was sold in 1871, and *Willie Wouldhave* coming into service in 1876. The *Northumberland* was later replaced by the *James Young* (1874) and the construction of the *Bedford* in 1886 left the *Tyne* as a reserve boat.

The *Tyne* can still be seen today – a memorial to the Tyne Lifeboat Institution, commemorating the service of the crews and the lifeboat builders. After six decades of life-saving she left her boathouse for the last time in 1894. She was pulled through crowd-lined streets and placed under a new canopy in Marine Parade on permanent public view. A fine boat with a fine record.

The sea could make the massive engineering work on the river piers look puny. In 1897 it broke through the North Pier battering down masonry which was built using stone blocks weighing up to 40 tons each on foundations 21 ft (6.6 m) deep.

Once within the piers, ships, like the Ann, *could still be driven onto the sands. On the left of the picture is the Groyne Light which was built to warn ships off and was first lit in 1882. The men in the foreground are looking at part of a ship which has been washed onto the beach.*

HAZARDS TO HAVENS:
New Piers and Lighthouses

Every North East shipowner knew that the safety of sailors and ships and the ultimate future of the Tyne and Wear's river ports depended on improving the rivers. Changing them from hazardous river mouths to harbours of refuge took over two centuries of ambitious engineering.

The River Wear Commissioners completed their first project, the South Pier, in 1730. This protected the river mouth and directed the ebb tide onto the shallow bar so as to scour a deeper channel. The pier had to be avoided by ships and so a wooden lighthouse was placed on the end as a warning as well as a marker to the entrance to the river.

The North Pier, built between 1787 and 1802, carried a more solid lighthouse. Jonathan Pickernell, the Commissioner's engineer, erected an elegant octagonal stone tower which stood 76 ft (22.8 m) high. He was always exploring the latest techniques for improving the river and, in 1797, introduced the earliest steam dredger to deepen the channel into the river.

No sooner was one set of works complete than shipowners would lobby for even greater improvements. In the 1840s and 1850s both piers and lighthouses had to be altered. The North Pier was lengthened and by an incredible feat of ingenuity the octagonal lighthouse, weighing 334 tons, was moved bodily 450 ft (135 m) along the new pier. The old wooden lighthouse was replaced with a tall lighthouse built of wrought iron. This iron lighthouse was removed in 1983 and can now be seen on the cliffs at Seaburn.

Despite the massive engineering works ships were still being wrecked as they entered the Wear. The South Pier Lighthouse keeper recorded 134 ships aground in 16 months of 1854/55. Ships – now built of iron and soon to be of steel – had been slowly increasing in size and needed a greater depth of water. The problem could only be solved by more extensive dredging and construction of huge breakwaters.

Starting in 1885, it took seventeen years to complete the 2,800 ft (840 m) long Roker Pier outside the old North Pier. Its red and white granite lighthouse was opened in 1903. After the south pier was started in 1890 the direction and force of waves changed. The waves became so damaging to the old piers that Pickernell's octagonal lighthouse had to be taken down and replaced with a tower of less weight.

The Tyne Improvement Commission was not formed until 1851, but it immediately began ambitious engineering work at the river mouth. Its plans included building huge protective piers with lighthouses, and dredging to remove obstructions and deepen the channel right up to Newcastle.

By the 1880s the river engineer felt the Tyne could be called a Harbour of Refuge. The dangerous bar had been dredged away to give a minimum depth in the river mouth of 20 ft (6 m). In 1881, 551 ships ran safely into the Tyne for shelter. But still more work was needed, for even after coming inside the piers, ships could still miss the safe channel. A light was needed and in 1882 Trinity House built a steel light on the groyne at South Shields.

The Victorian engineers also improved the system of lighthouses which helped ships to navigate along the North East coast. In 1871 Souter Lighthouse was opened on Lizard Point between the rivers Tyne and Wear, and in 1898

St Mary's Island Lighthouse, between the rivers Tyne and Blyth, came into operation. These were a great help to approaching ships; Souter, for example, could be seen from as far off as Whitby, and provided a light for ships making their final approach in to the Wear.

TREND-SETTING:
Tynemouth's Motor Lifeboat Rescues

No-one on Tyneside, or anywhere in Britain, had seen a lifeboat like the *J McConnell Hussey* in action. This lifeboat's rescue record whilst operating out of Tynemouth was to set the trend for the modern RNLI fleet.

When the *J McConnell Hussey*, the RNLI'S first experimental motor lifeboat, arrived on the Tyne in 1905 the local lifeboatmen were mistrustful of the new technology. For over 100 years all lifeboats had been rowed or sailed (steam engines had been too heavy and unreliable). Lieutenant Burton, an engineer, had been given charge of the new lifeboat and he had to find a crew of soldiers to demonstrate her capabilities. Once convinced of her seaworthiness the local lifeboatmen readily formed a crew. Apart from

The hospital steamer Rohilla *of Glasgow, wrecked at Whitby in 1914.*

the engine the 38 ft (11.4 m) boat was familiar enough to them; the *J McConnell Hussey* had begun her career as a pulling and sailing lifeboat.

After six years at Tynemouth the *J McConnell Hussey* was sent to Sunderland where she served until 1914. Her replacement on the Tyne was the purpose built, 40 ft (12 m), self-righting motor lifeboat, *Henry Vernon*. The boat still had auxiliary sails and oars. The *Henry Vernon* is renowned for her part in the *Rohilla* rescue which finally confirmed the value of motor propulsion for lifeboats.

In October 1914 the hospital ship *Rohilla* was steaming to Dunkirk to collect wounded soldiers, carrying aboard 220 crew and medical staff. It was wartime, so the lights on the coast of Britain were extinguished and at night ships navigated in darkness. Steaming into a gale, and with no lights to guide her, the *Rohilla* lost

The motor lifeboat Henry Vernon made RNLI history when her crew took her 40 miles to Whitby and rescued 50 people from the Rohilla after the local pulling lifeboat was disabled. The 40 ft (12 m) self-righting boat also served at Sunderland.

her way and went aground on the rocks off Whitby harbour.

Four lifeboats, including one summoned from the Tees, attempted to reach the ship. Three were beaten back by the ferocity of the seas. The remaining boat made two trips, collecting 35 people, but was then too battered to put to sea again. It was clear that traditional pulling and sailing lifeboats could not contend with the conditions and a telephone message was sent to Tynemouth. The *Henry Vernon* took all night to cover the 45 miles to Whitby. She entered the harbour, took on oil, and as dawn broke put out to sea to rescue those left aboard the *Rohilla*. The seas were breaking right over the stricken *Rohilla* and soon the capabilities of the motor lifeboat were apparent. She worked to seaward of the ship, an almost impossible task for a sailing boat, and then discharging oil on the waters to calm them dropped down to

A salvage team being pulled back from the Cairnglen. *The crew and cargo were safely brought ashore after the ship broke her back on rocks at Marsden.*

leeward of the *Rohilla*. Despite being submerged by the huge seas as they came over the *Rohilla* the lifeboat took off the remaining 50 people.

The rescue remains one of the great achievements of the RNLI and the boat superintendent and the coxswain were both awarded the Institution's gold medals for conspicuous gallantry.

By the end of 1918 the *Henry Vernon* had saved 206 lives. She was then transferred to Sunderland and, in the quieter years of peace, saved a further 64 lives before leaving the station in 1935.

The Second World War brought further demands on the services of both lifeboats and shore rescue teams. At times the secrecy of war prevented immediate public recognition of their achievements – a member of South Shields Volunteer Life Brigade had to wait until the war ended to be awarded the British Empire Medal for a rescue he made from the *Cairnglen* in 1940.

In October 1940, carrying a cargo of wheat, bacon, engines and tyres from Canada, the *Cairnglen* had safely reached the North East coast. But her skipper misinterpreted the channel-marking buoys for the Tyne and ran her on to the rocks at Marsden. The increasingly heavy seas forced her further ashore until the hull was pierced and her back broken by the rocks. On the cliff tops the Roker and South Shields Volunteer Life Brigades joined forces to bring ashore by breeches buoy the 49 man crew. As the weather moderated their breeches buoys carried salvage experts across to the vessel and much of the *Cairnglen*'s cargo was saved. Today parts of the wreck are still visible and are regularly visited by local divers. A porthole from the wreck is on display in Souter Lighthouse.

ON COURSE FOR THE MODERN WORLD

The eighteenth century fishermen who once rowed their cobles to the aid of so many sailing ships would barely recognise today's rivers or rescue services. Inshore fishing has declined and the heavy industries of Victorian Tyneside and Wearside have all but disappeared. The docks are either filled in or almost empty and most of the shipyards have gone along with the colliers, sailing ships and much of the metal-hulled British merchant fleet. Container ships have arrived; one modern ship with just a handful of crew could move as much cargo in half the time as half a dozen tramp steamers.

After the 1914-1918 War the Tyne Lifeboat Institution rarely launched their boats, the *Tom Perry*, *Willie Wouldhave*, *Bedford* and *James Young*. The sailing ships which had most needed them were almost extinct. In 1900 Britain's sailing merchant ships numbered around one million but by 1939 only 500 ships remained. The steamships which replaced sail had powerful engines to keep them out of danger and the North East harbours had been made deep and safe.

The local Tyne Lifeboat Institution tried to streamline their fleet. First an engine was fitted in the *Bedford* to make her swifter and to reduce the number of crew needed. In 1936, the *James Young* was sold. But the Tyne Lifeboat Institution's boats, when compared with the RNLI motor lifeboats, were becoming obsolete. They had not attended a wreck since 1937 and no one was particularly concerned when the *James Young* and the *Willie Wouldhave* were accidentally destroyed – one by a wartime bomb and the other by fire. The *Bedford* stood idle in her boathouse until 1968 when she was

WRECKS AND RESCUES

Coastguards and Volunteer Life Brigadesmen set up a breeches buoy to the Adelfotis *which ran aground at the Groyne Light, January 20 1963.*

A crewman is rescued by breeches buoy from the Adelfotis.

finally taken to Exeter Maritime Museum.

In contrast, RNLI stations at Tynemouth and Sunderland remain operational today, adapting to the needs of modern shipping as the RNLI modernised its lifeboats and improved its rescue service.

After the Second World War the RNLI concentrated on upgrading its fleet. Motor lifeboats were introduced everywhere, the last sailing boat going out of commission at Whitby in 1956. New designs were introduced with improved self-righting capabilities and greater off-shore range. The lifeboat's efficiency was increased by the introduction of radio communications enabling lifeboatmen to talk to vessels in distress and to be coordinated by the coastguard who have links with rescue helicopters. The value of coordinated team work learnt so clearly back in 1861 with the rescue of the *Fowlis* is just as important today.

While merchant ships have become far fewer the number of leisure craft has mushroomed. In the 1960s Inshore Lifeboats (ILB), usually inflatables, were introduced. These are kept busy ensuring the safety of swimmers, wind-surfers, yachtspeople and divers, and on many stations the Inshore Lifeboats have replaced the all-weather lifeboats.

Around the coasts of Britain the Volunteer Life Brigades have now mostly disappeared, disbanding or amalgamating with the Auxiliary Coastguards. Only on the Tyne and Wear do they still exist, the Volunteer Life Brigades at Tynemouth, South Shields and Roker are still carrying on their proud tradition. The last rescue by the North East brigades was on 20th January in 1963. The South Shields and Sunderland volunteers worked together to bring 23 men ashore from the Lebanese ship *Adelfotis II* which went aground by the Groyne Light in the Tyne. The ship was rolling heavily and many helpers were needed to haul the breeches buoy ashore.

DIVING INTO THE PAST

Evidence of the wrecks and rescues can be seen in the Volunteer Life Brigade Watch Houses when they open their doors to the public. For divers there is also the chance to explore numerous wrecks in the waters off the Tyne and the Wear.

Most of the known diving sites are metal ships lost in this century. Such is the power of the North Sea that before long, wrecks in exposed positions are reduced to no more than their boilers, engines or a set of ribs. Many North East shipwrecks have been stripped for salvage or, more recently, by souvenir hunting divers.

Wrecks of wooden sailing ships are more difficult to find, surviving only by being buried or as objects scattered across the seabed. Yet in the last millennium thousands of the ships working out of Tyne and Wear must have been lost. A chance discovery by a diver could throw fresh light on the great maritime history of the two rivers. Until then we can only wonder at the incredible maritime secrets which are hidden in the seabed of the North East.

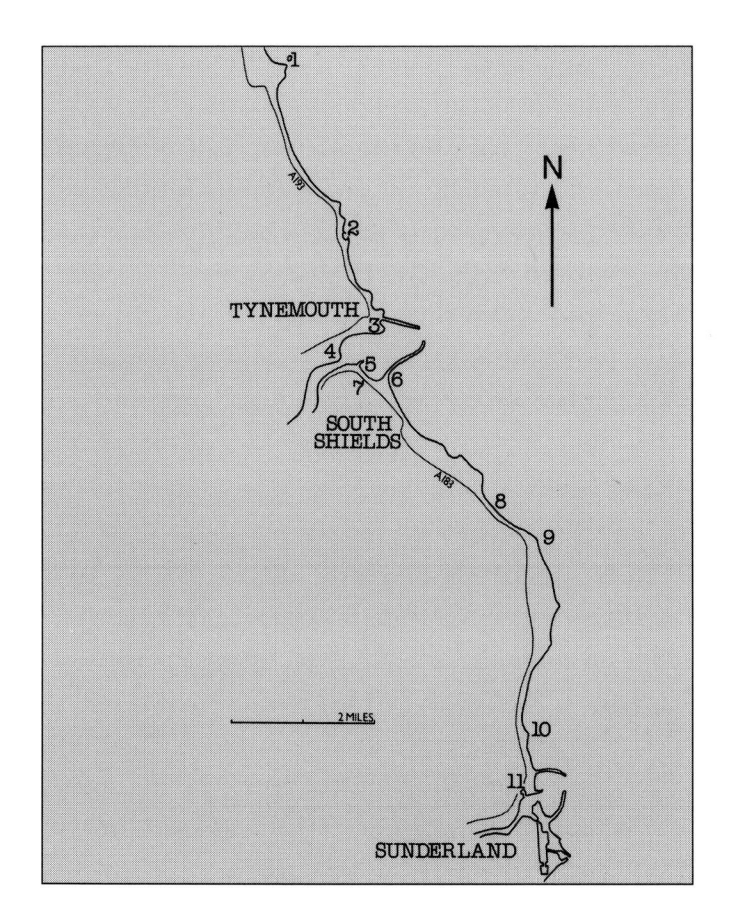

LOOKING AROUND

1. St Mary's Lighthouse.

The 126 ft (40 m) high lighthouse can be reached on foot at low tide via a causeway from the headland car park. Built for Trinity House Newcastle, it operated from 1898 to 1984. Inside there are displays on the light's history and the island's wildlife, and visitors may climb to the lantern house.

2. Cullercoats Volunteer Life Brigade Watch House.

From Whitley Bay the Promenade leads south along the cliff top to Tynemouth. In Cullercoats the road passes the small stone Watch House which stands on the cliff edge above the bay in which the lifeboat house can be seen. On the opposite side of the road is a garage which once housed the Life-saving Apparatus.

3. Tynemouth.

The Tyne Piers (built 1856-1908) are best seen from the car park by the old Spanish Battery, reached via Pier Road. The remains of the Castle and Priory can be seen on the high headland to the north. It was the site of a 79 ft high stone lighthouse from 1664-1898 whose light comprised a coal fire. The sailing club in the bay below occupies the site of the RNLI's first Tyne lifeboat station which opened in 1862.

The Volunteer Life Brigade Watch House, which is regularly opened to the public, is a treasure-house of Brigade and wreck memorabilia. At low tide the notorious Black Middens Rocks can be overlooked from the riverside promenade.

4. The High and Low Lights, North Shields.

Look from the High Light (off Dockwray

Square, above the Fishquay) across the roof of the Low Light and your view is straight between the piers of the river mouth. The alignment of these and earlier 'leading lights' have guided sailors into the Tyne since 1536. The present towers were opened in 1810.

5. Groyne Light, South Shields.

The Groyne Light was built in 1882 by Trinity House, Newcastle. It can be reached from the car park at the north end of Harbour Drive which also gives a sea-level view of the piers, the Tynemouth headland with the Volunteer Life Brigade Watch House, the High and Low Lights and the RNLI lifeboat station at North Shields.

6. South Shields Volunteer Life Brigade Watch House.

The Watch House, built in 1886, stands on the landward end of the South Pier. It is opened to the public and the display includes rockets and breeches buoys used to rescue crews from ships ashore. Most were wrecked either on the outside of the pier or on the sands which run north to the Groyne Light.

7. Tyne Lifeboat.

First launched in 1833 this sturdy lifeboat was in service for sixty years before being placed on public view in Marine Parade (leading inland from the pier) in 1894. She is the same design as the *Original* lifeboat built by Greathead in 1789. Wrecks were once so numerous that there were four such lifeboats at work on the Tyne together.

8. Marsden.

The A183 follows the coast south to Sunderland. The rugged rock stacks visible from the roadside car park at Marsden show the hard climb faced by any sailor unfortunate enough to be wrecked beneath the cliffs.

9. Souter Lighthouse.

The tower stands 153 ft (46 m) above sea level and is visible from Whitby. Opened in 1871 it was closed in 1988 and is now owned by the National Trust. In addition to the lighthouse, with its full machinery, visitors can see how the keepers and their families lived in the adjoining cottages.

10. Roker Lighthouse, Seaburn.

The lighthouse was moved to the cliff top at Seaburn from the South Pier at Sunderland in 1983. It was built in 1856 by Meik, the River Wear Engineer, using wrought iron plates around a cast iron staircase.

11. Roker Volunteer Life Brigade Watch House.

The new Watch House, built in 1905, overlooks the mouth of the Wear from the top of Pier View Road. It contains wreck and Brigade memorabilia and is opened to the public. From the promenade below it is possible to walk along the North Pier to the 150 ft (45 m) high, red and white granite lighthouse which started work in 1903.

FURTHER READING

Collings, P. The Illustrated Dictionary of North East Shipwrecks
Osler, A. 1990 Mr. Greathead's Lifeboats
Whitaker, B. 1979 Skuetender Lifeboat
Whitaker, B. 1980 South Shields Volunteer Life Brigade
Whitaker, B. 1980 Tynemouth Volunteer Life Brigade

Further information about the RNLI can be obtained from:

The Director
RNLI
West Quay Road
Poole
Dorset
BH15 1HZ
Tel (0202) 671 133

The RNLI is a registered charity and funded entirely by voluntary contributions.

WRECKS AND RESCUES

Modern day rescues.